CW00447972

WATCHMEN PORTRAITS

WATCHMEN PORTRAITS
9781848560697

Published by
Titan Books
A division of
Titan Publishing Group Ltd
144 Southwark St
London
SE1 0UP

First edition January 2009
10 9 8 7 6 5 4 3 2 1

Visit our website:
WWW.TITANBOOKS.COM

WATCHMEN

PORTRAITS

PHOTOGRAPHY BY
CLAY ENOS

FOREWORD BY
ZACK SNYDER

TITAN BOOKS

'm haunted by faces. On the most basic level they're the point where humans make thei strongest emotional connection with one another My obsession comes from a lifelong practice o photography, trying to coax out the stories each face has to tell. The stories can come from the quirky wrinkle in a crooked smile, the hard shadow tha accentuates to near grotesqueness a perfect bone structure, or the deeply rutted forehead compressing in anguish above raised brows — but most of all you can always find them in the eyes if you work a t hard enough.

Clay Enos is haunted by faces, too. He collects hem; always has. That's why when we hired him as he unit still photographer on *Watchmen* he went about his duties with his usual enthusiasm and aesthetic expertise. It also meant that withou bothering to mention it to anyone, he began compiling he stunning collection of images you have here.

t was fascinating to see him lay out all the photos for selection, like a vast mosaic on the floor, poring over each one and searching for that intangible something that struck just the right chord inside him. Watching someone work like that is an awesome experience, and I count myself lucky to be able to work with somebody I value as a friend and whom also respect as an artist.

look at this volume as part yearbook and part ar book. In one sense, this is a touching record of ar enormous undertaking and the people who gave so much of themselves for it over many arduous months. Not only do these pages immortalize ndividual cast and crewmembers, but they also celebrate in particular the exceptional work of ou talented costume, hair, and make-up departments

But even beyond that, the photos of the actors ir costume capture something more. What at first glance simply might appear to be an extra dressed up as a general for a day, reveals on closer study the decades of a career spent in uniform. An actor ir ights and a hood becomes a masked vigilante from a bygone age that could have been. Another is a world leader with Armageddon bearing down or him. Each image is a complete narrative of ar entirely other lifetime.

That's what we try to convey over the course of ar entire feature film, but Clay's done it here in each and every frame.

Zack Snyde

WATCHMENPORTRAITS

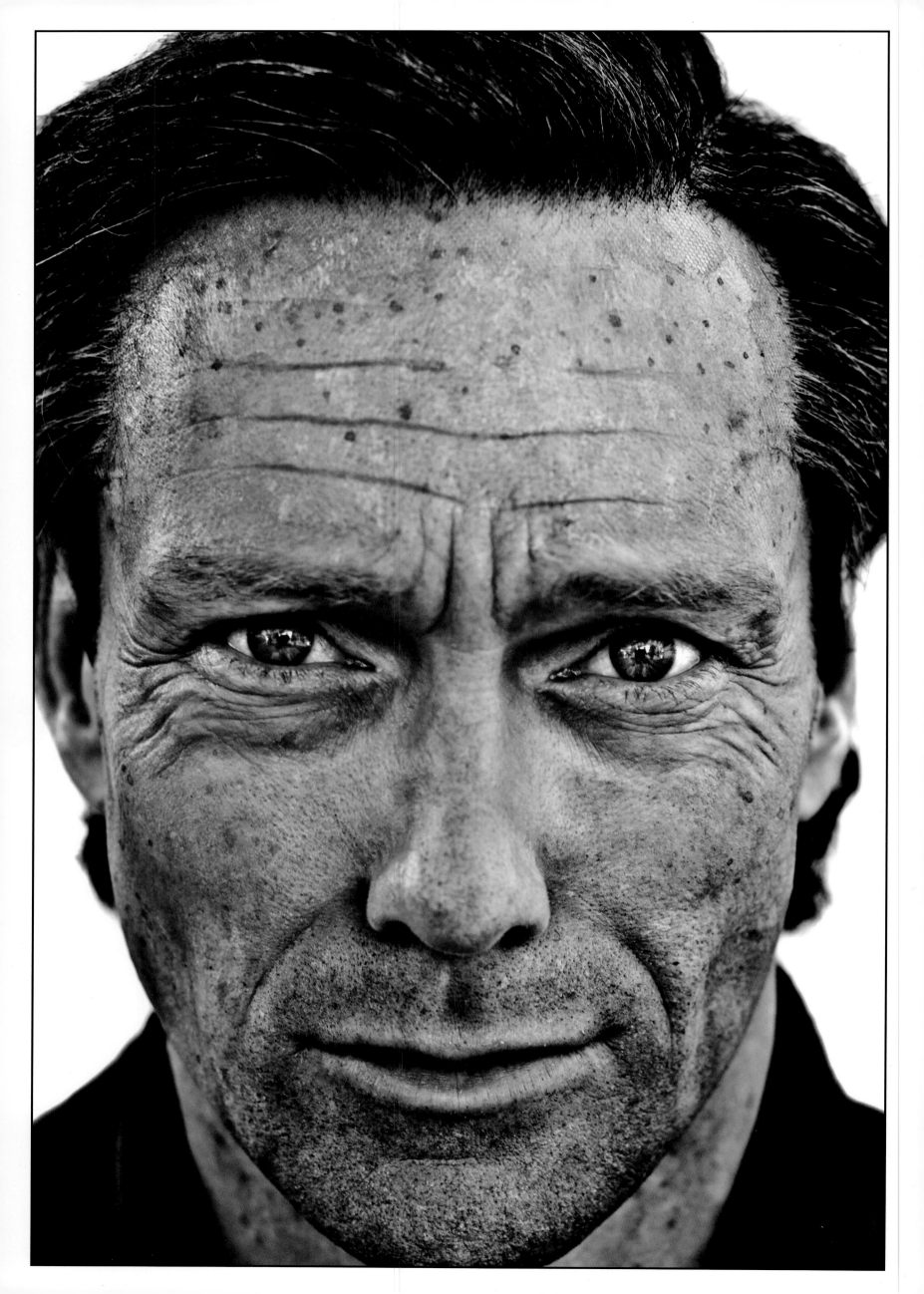

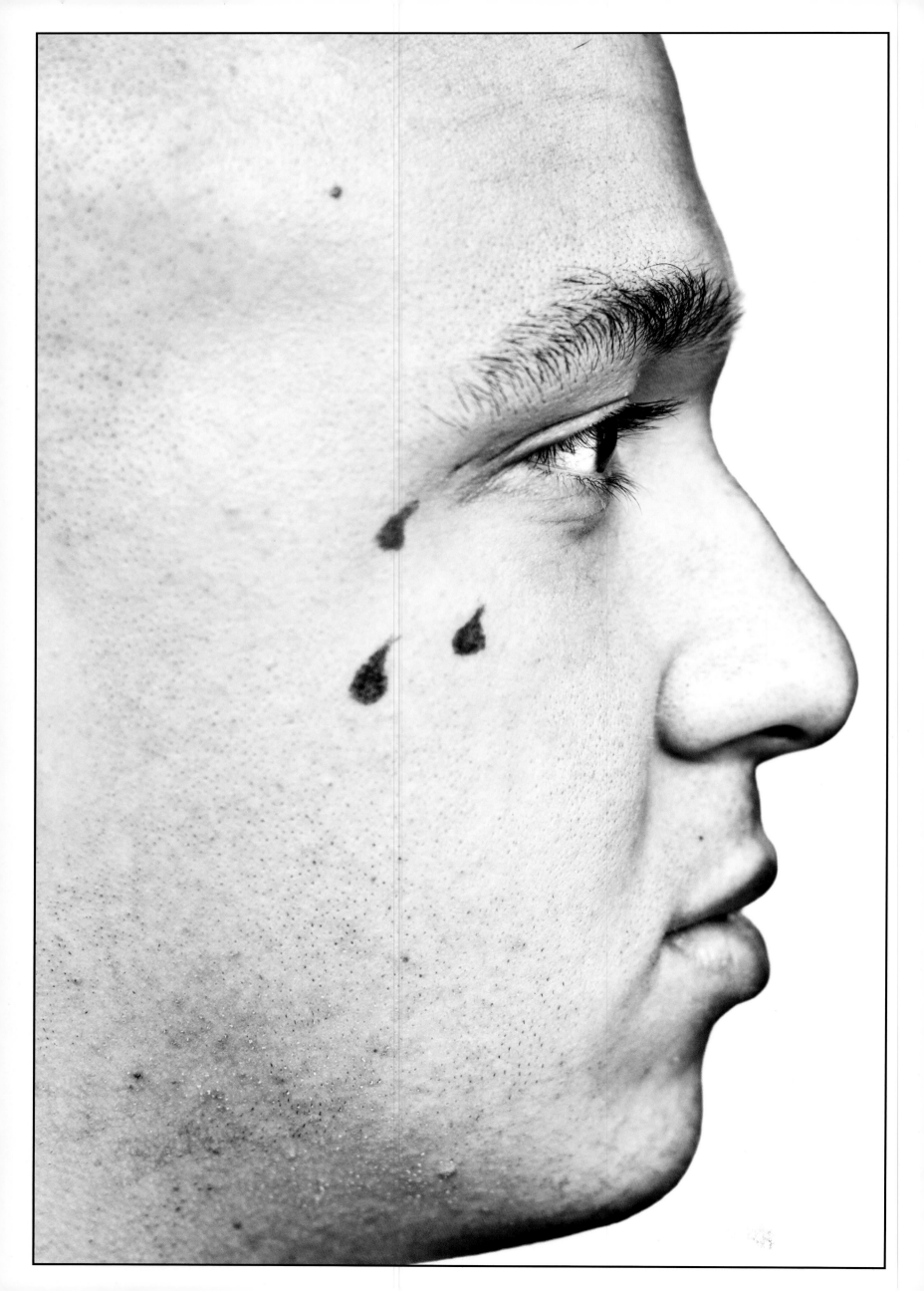

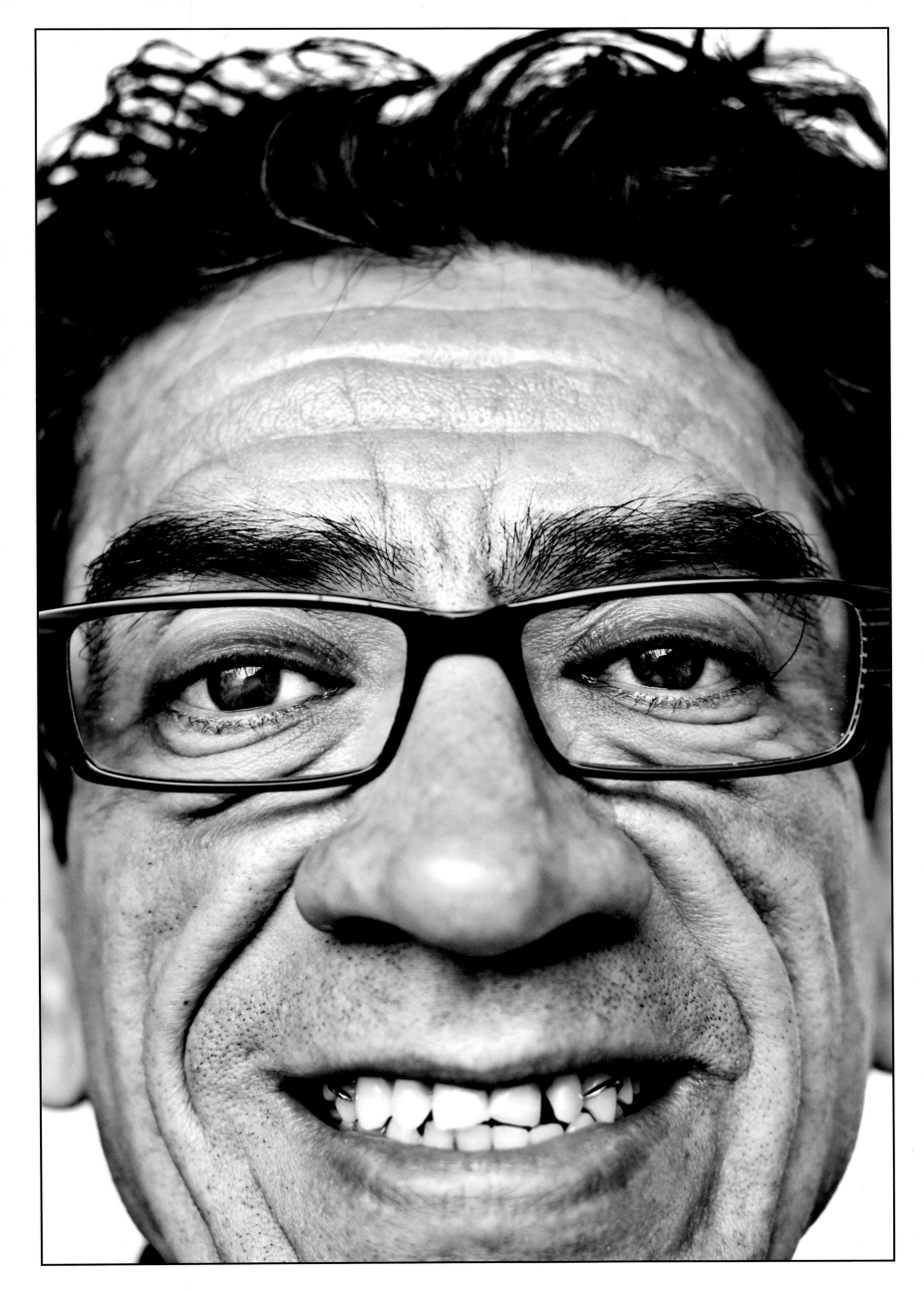

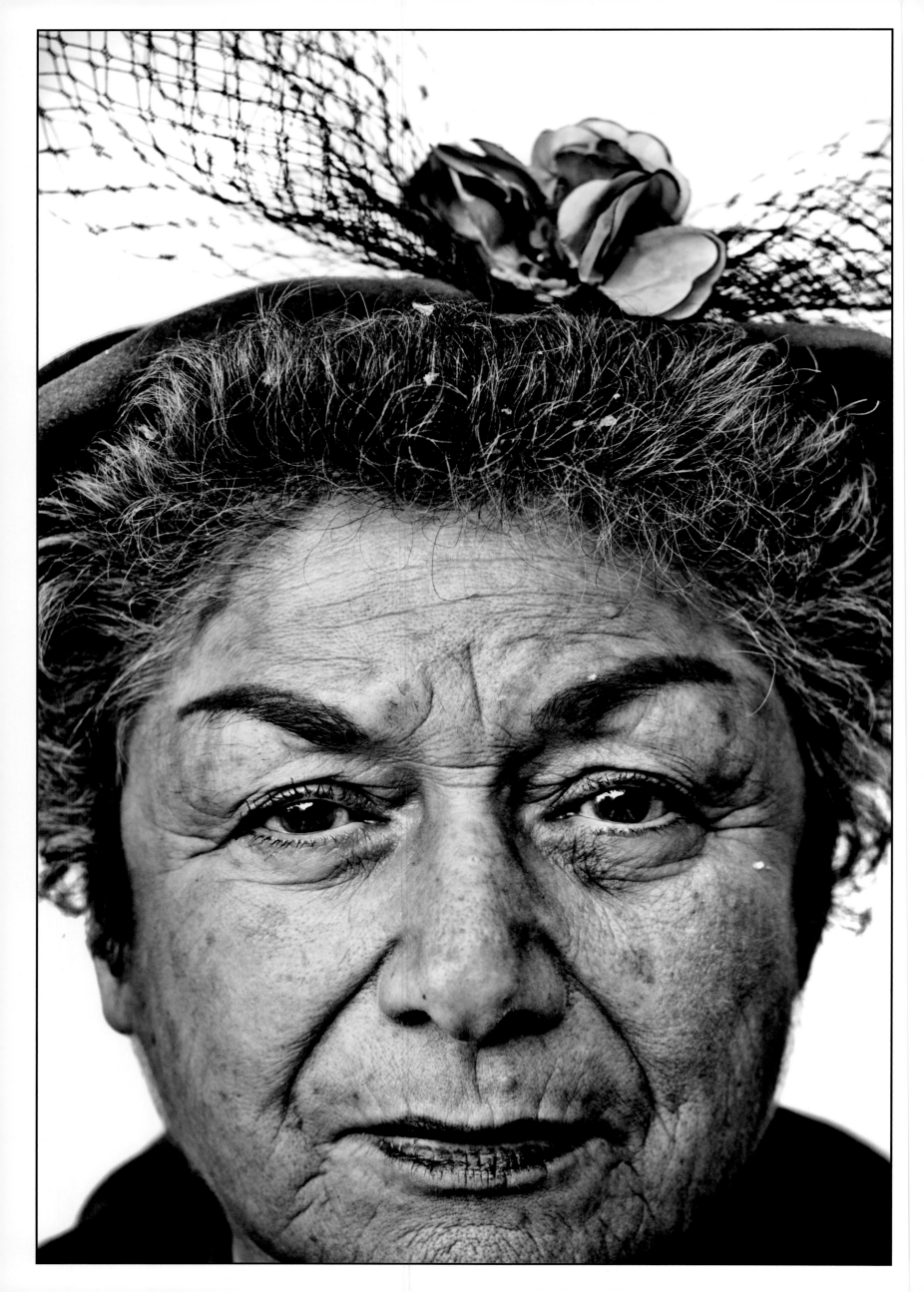

Sex Scandal Outs Silhouette From Minutemen

Dames' Embrace Shocker!
Disgraced Silhouette Forced to Resign

By WILLIAM BALL
Special to The New York Gazette

After much continuing public outcry at the scandalous behaviour of Silhouette on V-Day, the Watchmen crime fighting group have expelled her from their ranks. The shocking picture of Silhouette and an unidentified Nurse kissing in full view of thousands of celebrating New Yorkers, taken in Times Square on V-Day, has exposed her as a "lesbian." New Yorkers across the country have been outraged at the decency and moral values of our nation.

Silhouette was an original member of The Minutemen. Joining in 1939, Successfully fighting crime for most of her career, she left her native country due to the rise of Nazism in Austria, she immigrated to New York. A Jew, Ursula a.k.a. Silhouette made a new home on the Lower East Side. After several years floating from various part time jobs, she quit the regular work force to soon fight as a crime fighter in the tough neighborhoods bordering the Waterfront.

Shortly there after, she joined a costumed vigilante group known as The Minutemen.

Plan Antagonizes Workers

By LEON BUCKLEY
Special to The New York Gazette

The death toll from a massive

of India, officials said more than 1000 injured ... and that the numbers of both the dead and injured would surely rise once more rescue investigation has been done in

Silk Spectre, the only other female crime fighter. It is now speculated that the two sexy vigilantes, where at one time "lesbian lovers". An unnamed source suggested that the illicit affair didn't last long. Rumours suggested Spectre's Polish origins or perhaps it was jealousy over Silk Spectre's blossoming movie career that caused the breakup. In 1965, Silhouette attended the Retirement Party for Silk Spectre held at the new Watchmen headquarters from the same female companion from the Time Square incident

The shocking picture of Silhouette and an unidentified Nurse kissing in full view of thousands of celebrating New Yorkers, taken in Times Square on V-Day, has exposed many Americans across the country the decency and moral values of our nation. An original member of The Minutemen to join The Watchmen. Successfully fighting crime for most of her career.

Born Ursula Zandt in Austria, she left her native country due to the rise of Nazism and immigrated to New York. A Jew, Ursula a.k.a. Silhouette made a new home on the Lower East Side. She quit the regular work force to soon fight as a crime fighter in the tough neighborhoods bordering the Lower East Side and joined a costumed vigilante group known as The Minutemen.

Silhouette's public smooch leads to scandal and dismissal.

Dispute Nearing End

(handwritten) *...girlfriend murdered ... stuffed in mouth*

(handwritten) *Cartkowste*

PYRAMID
A NEW WORLD DELIVERED

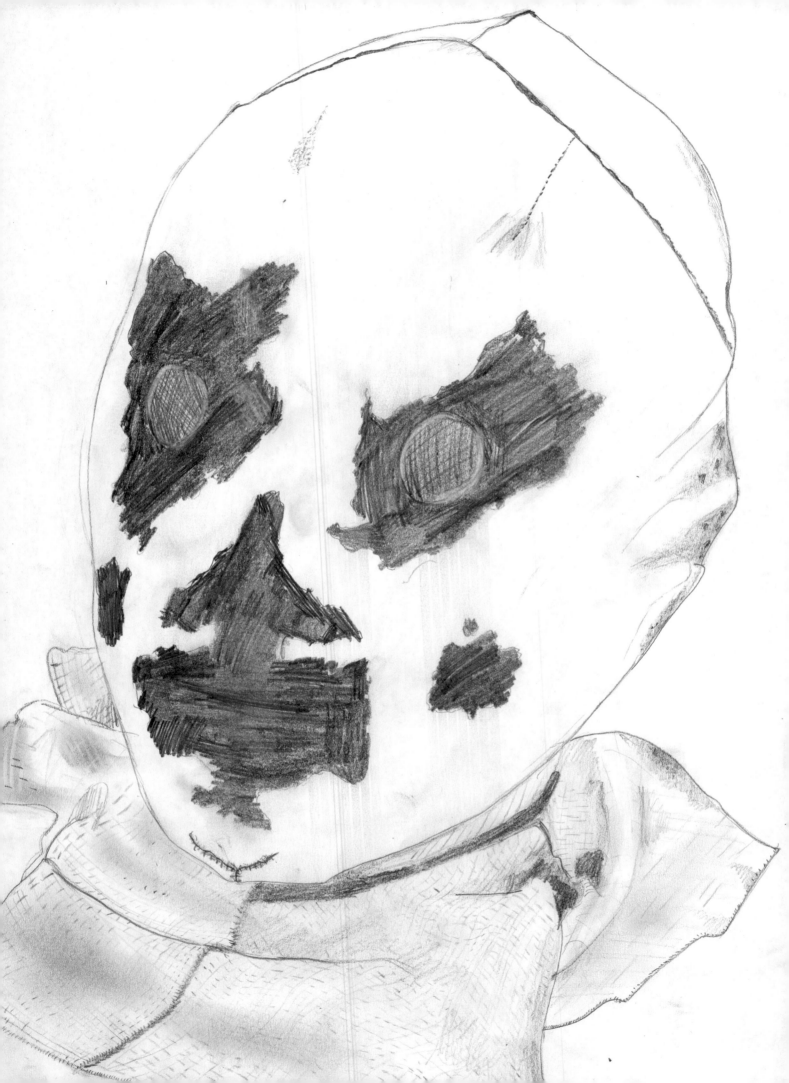

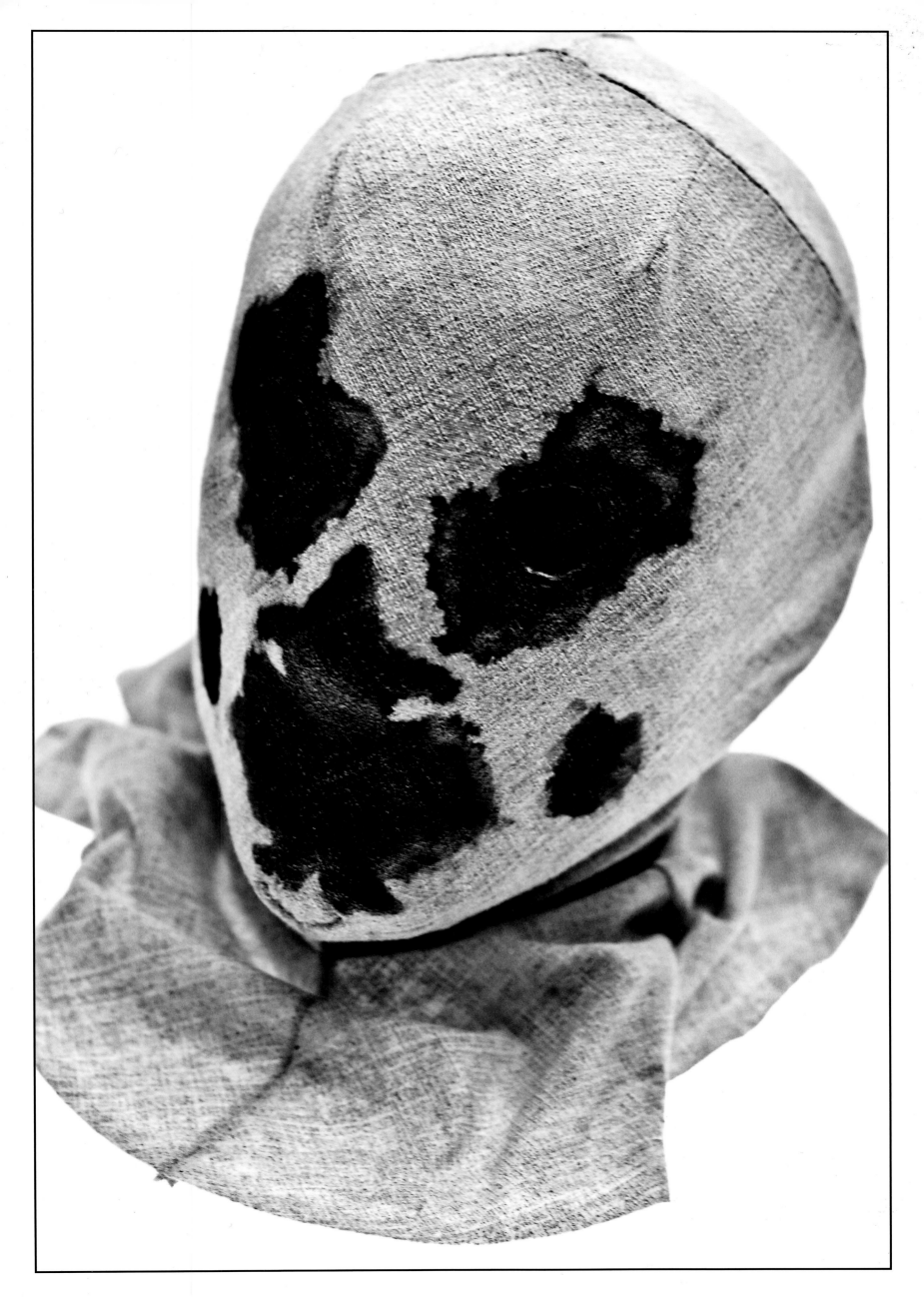

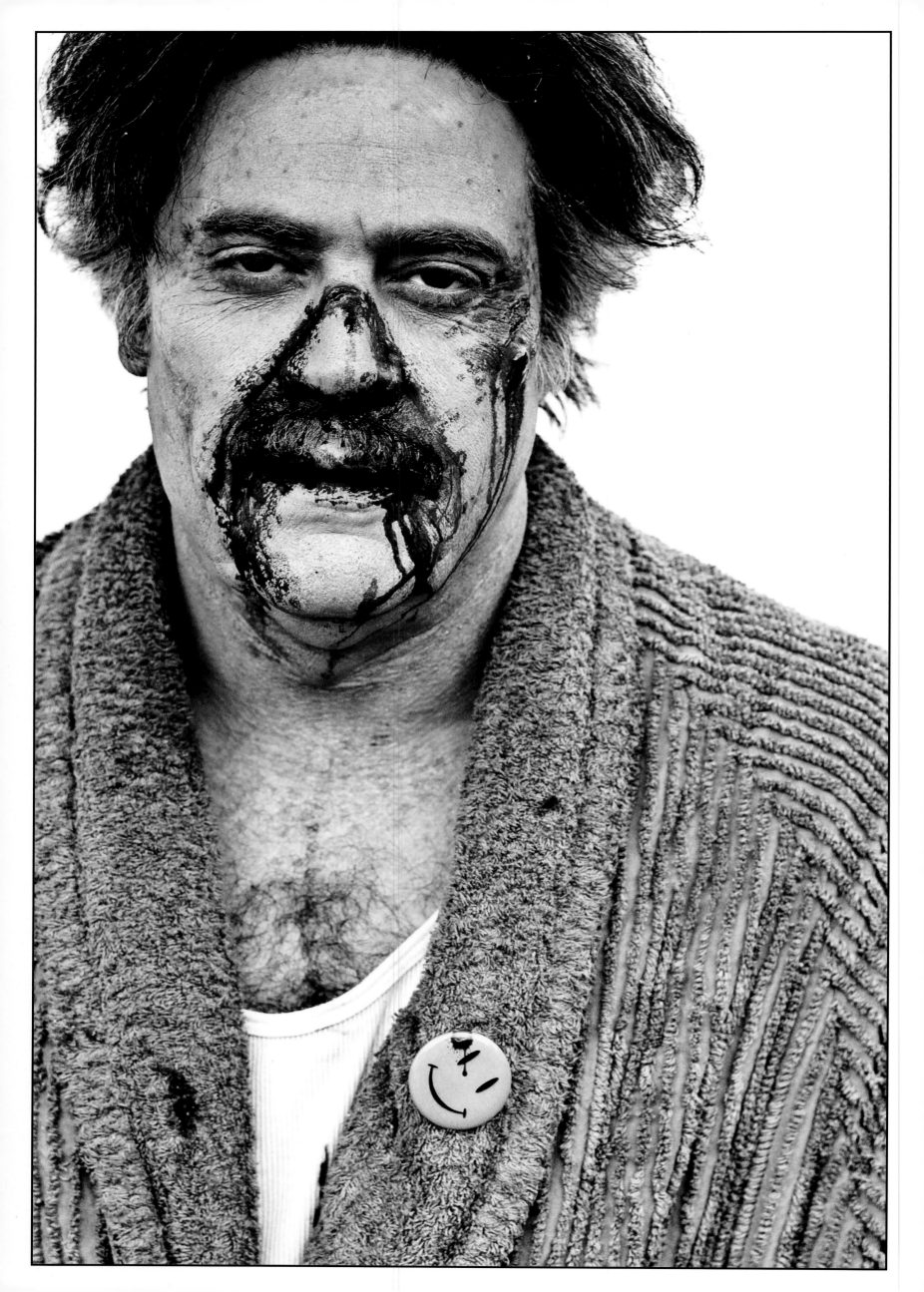

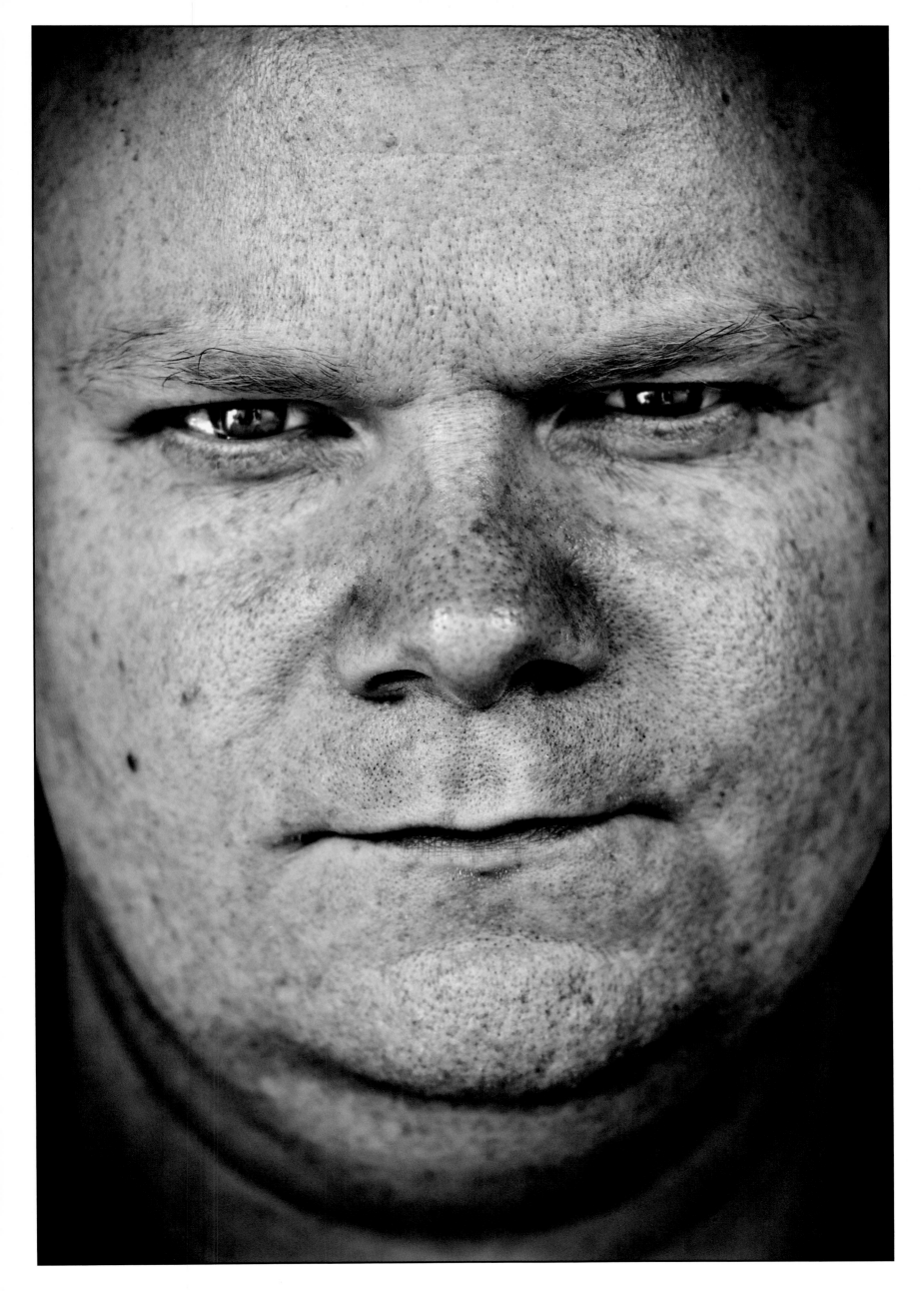

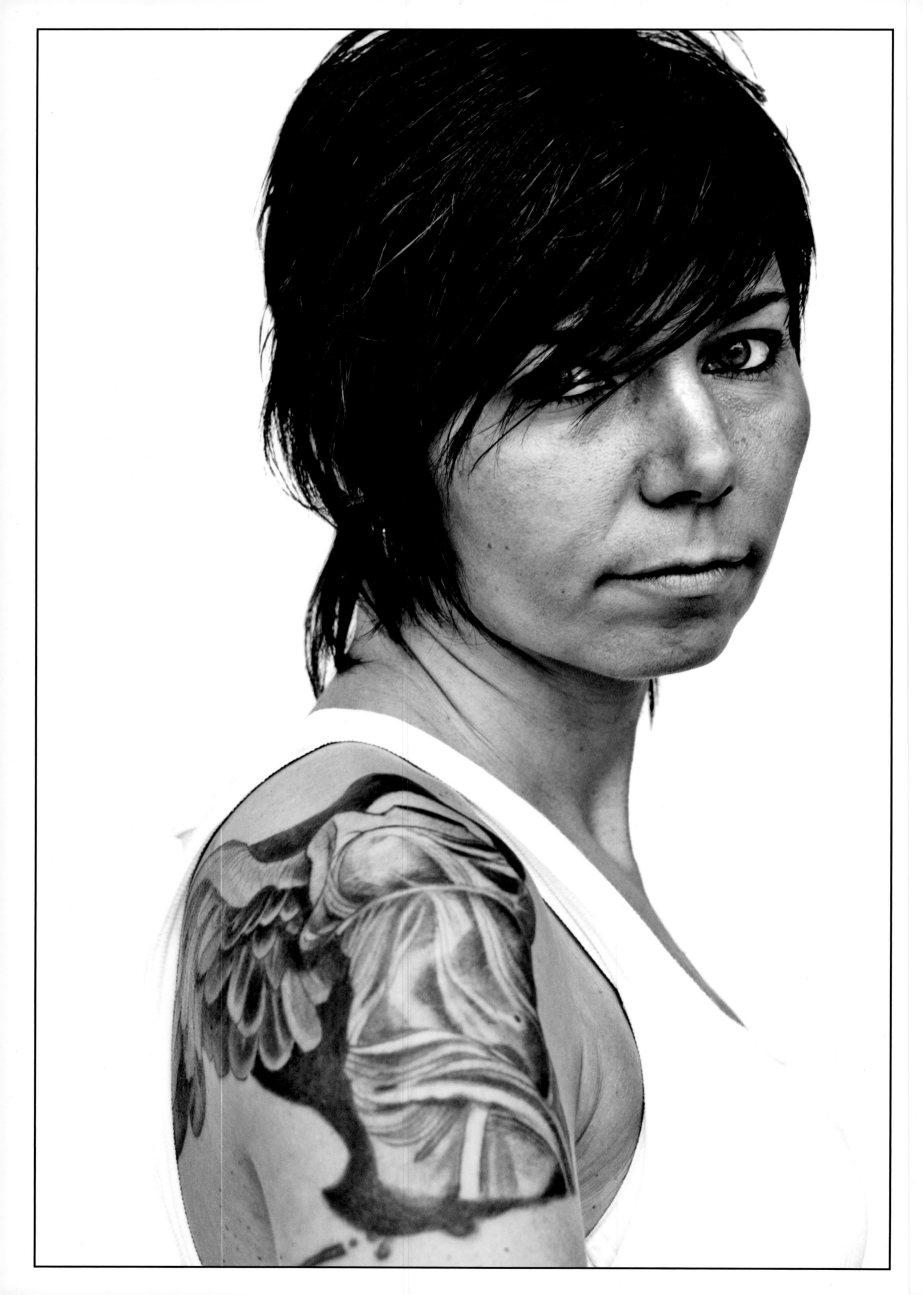

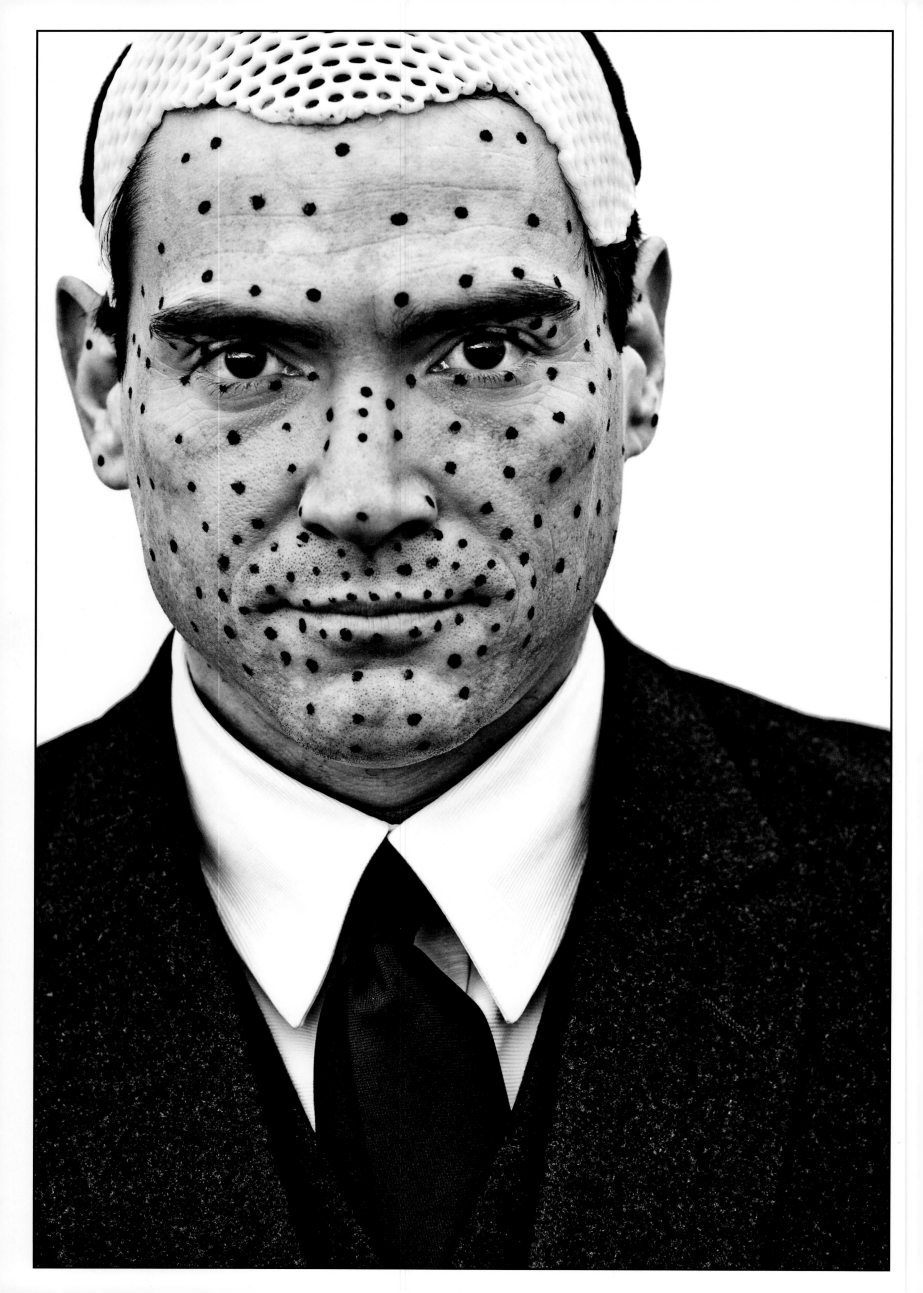

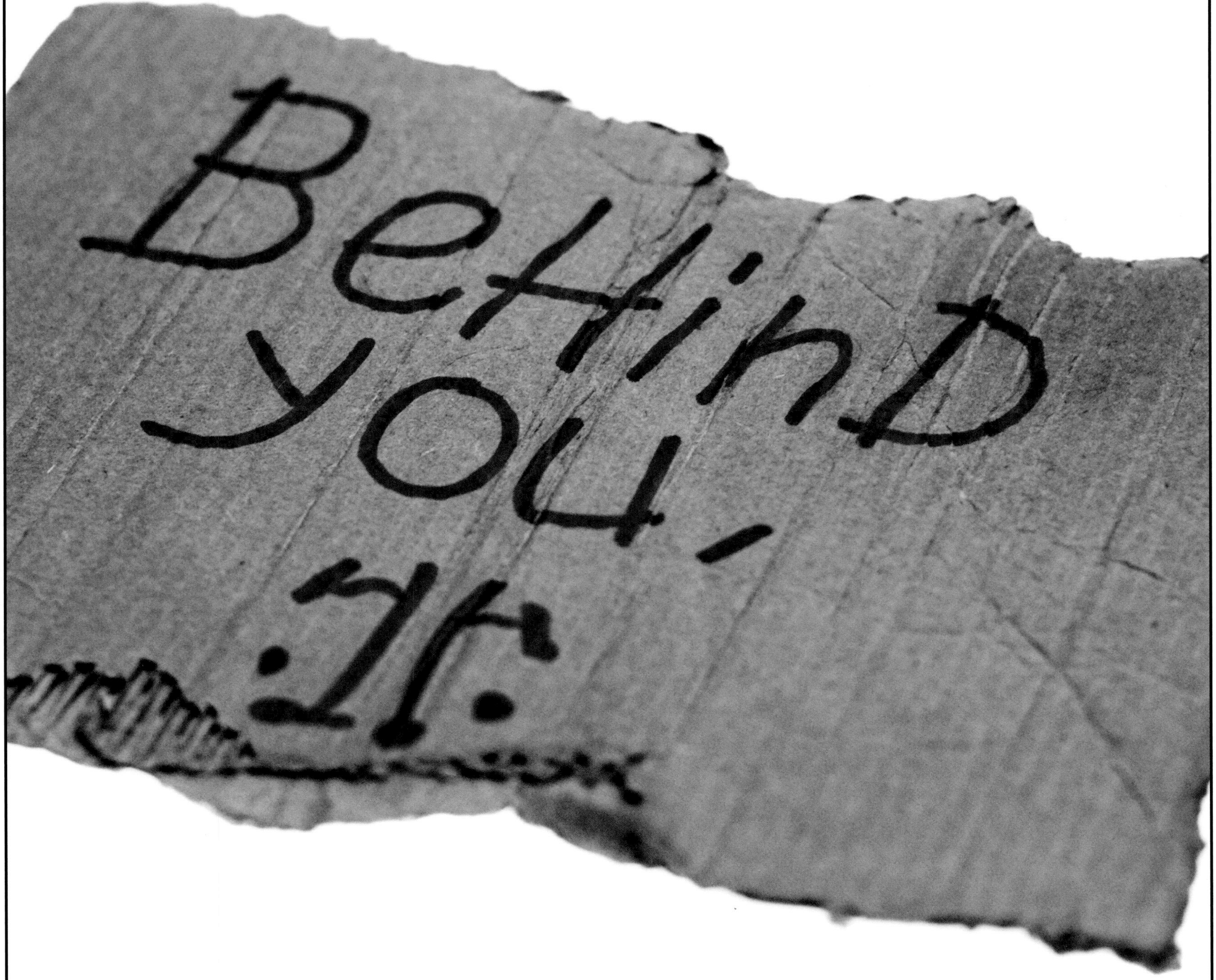

BeHinD
you

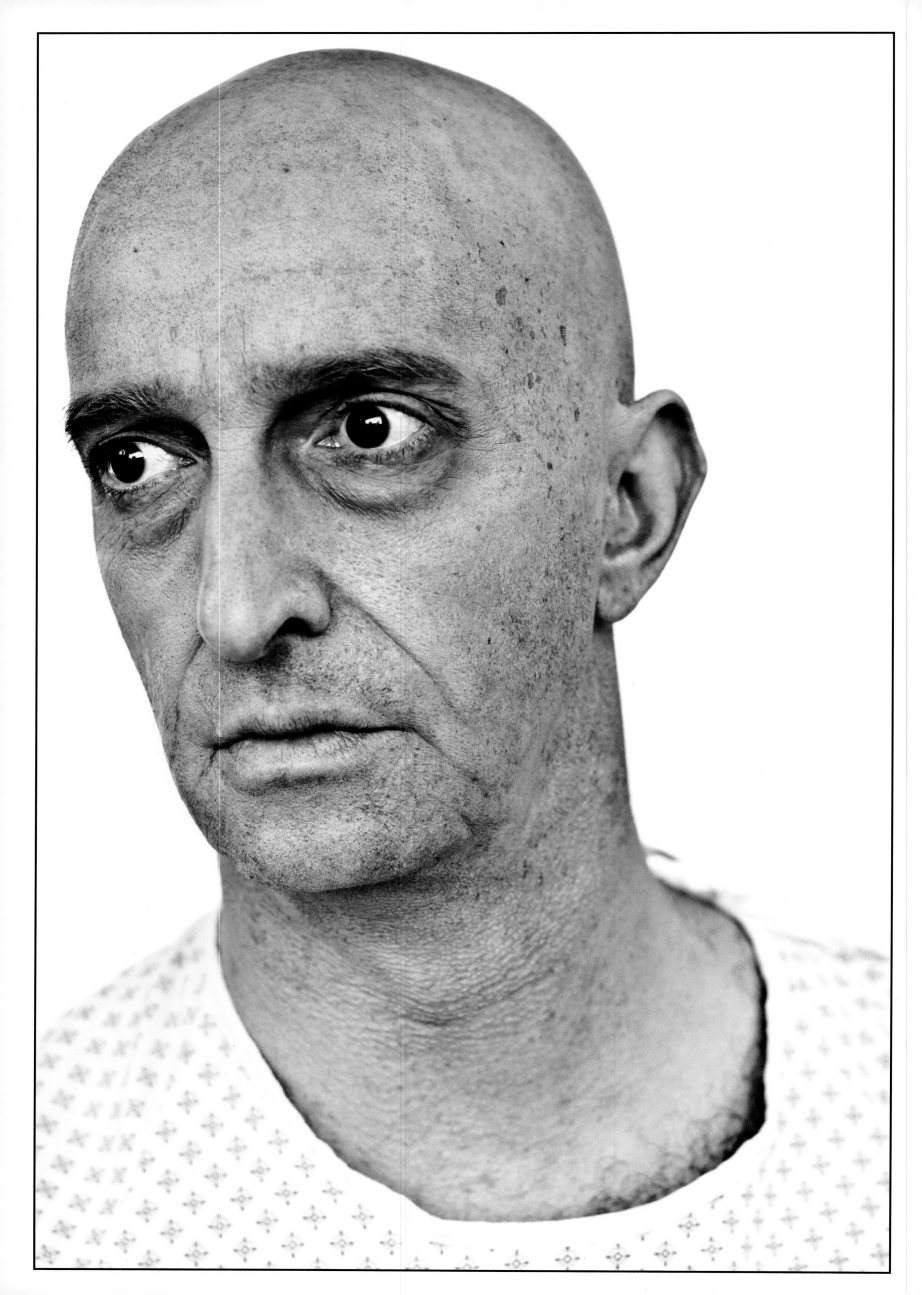

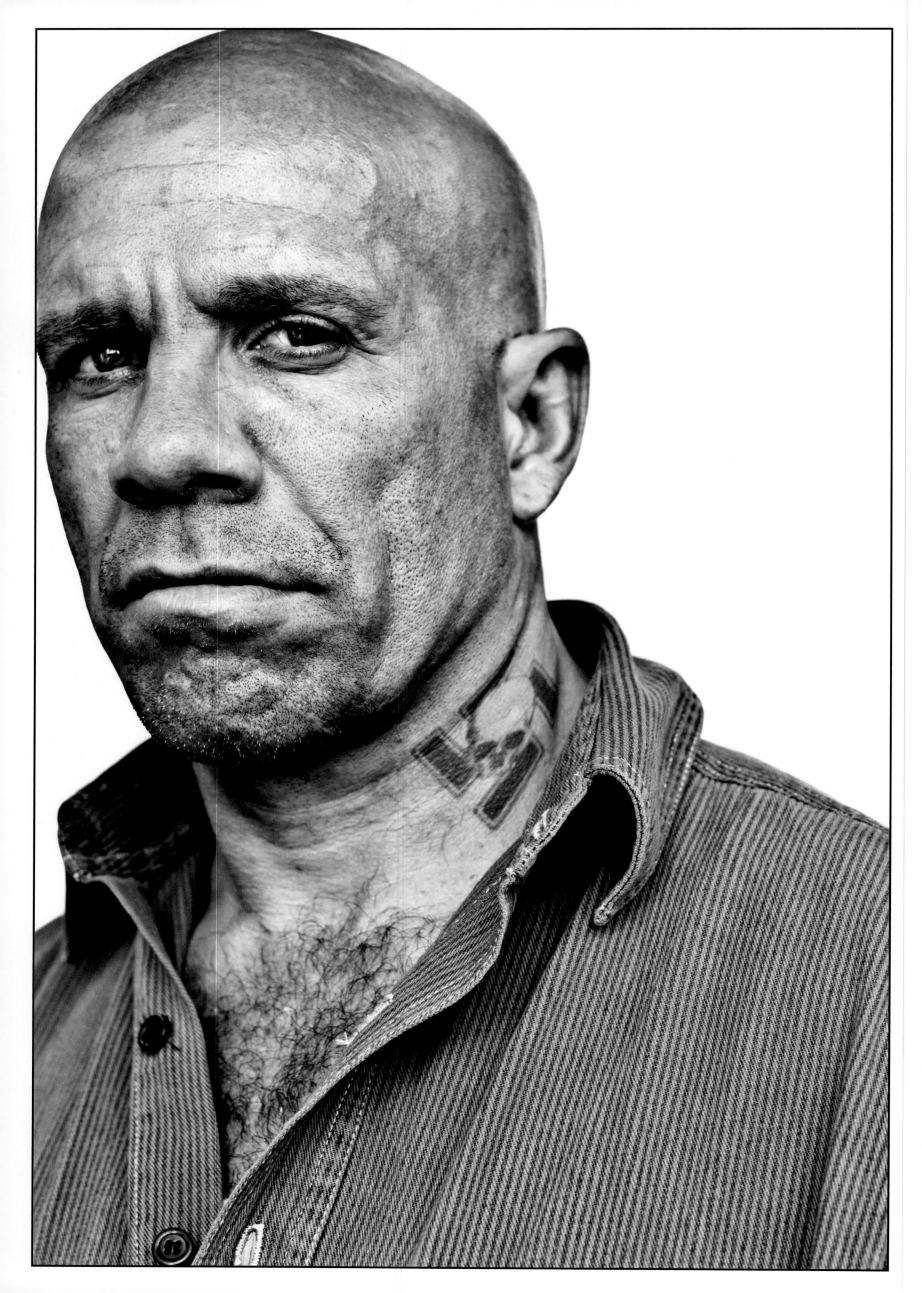

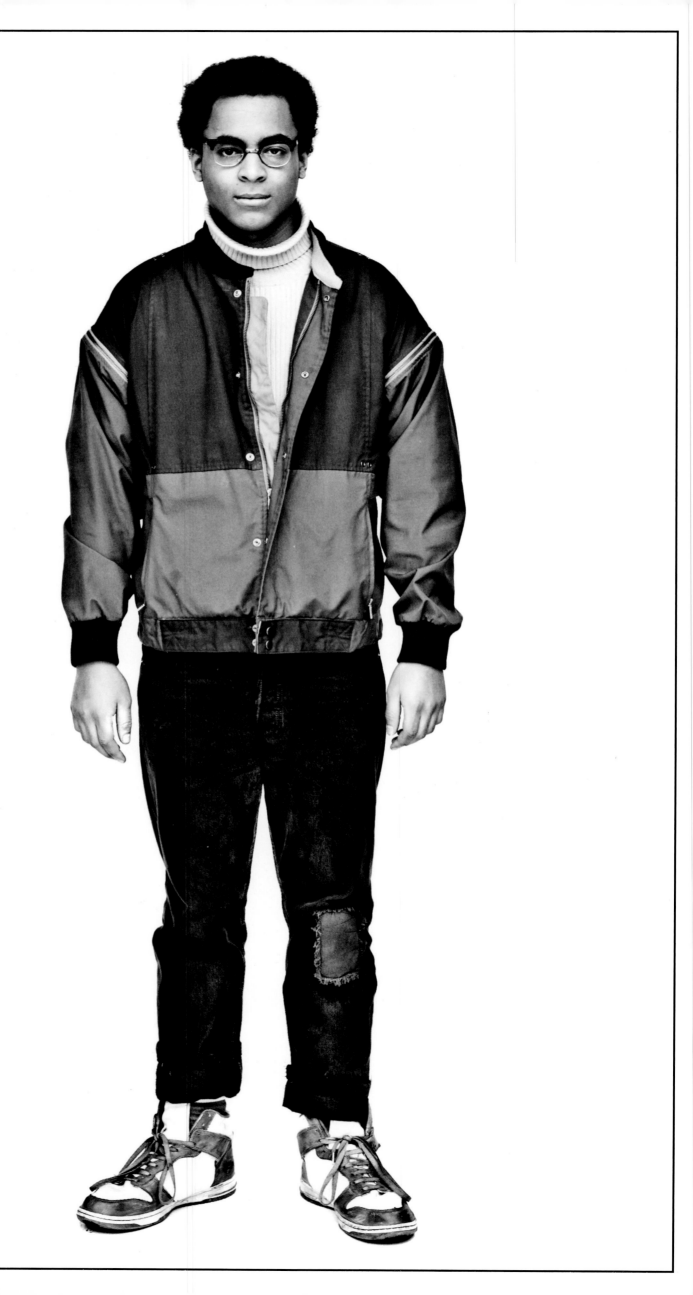

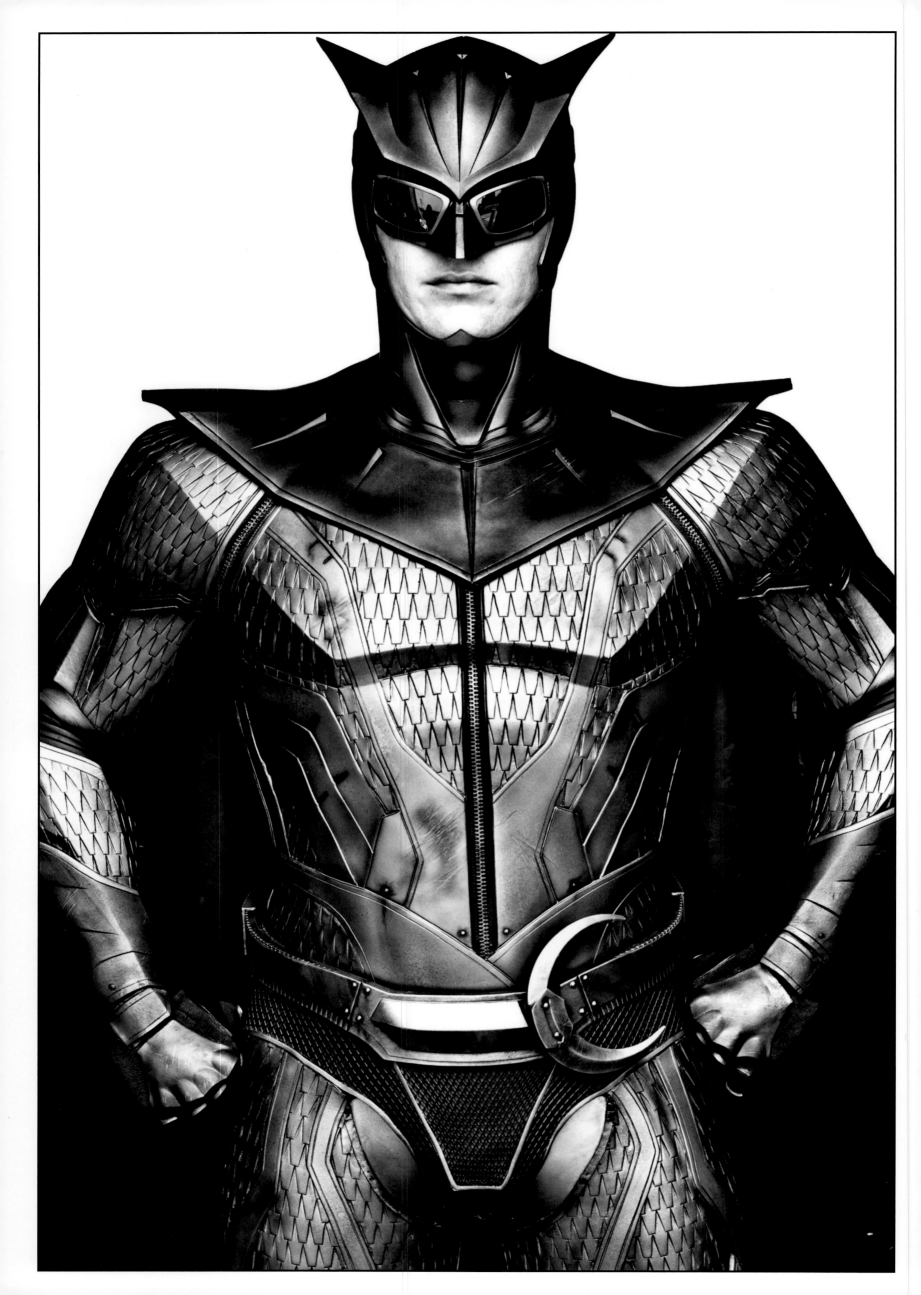

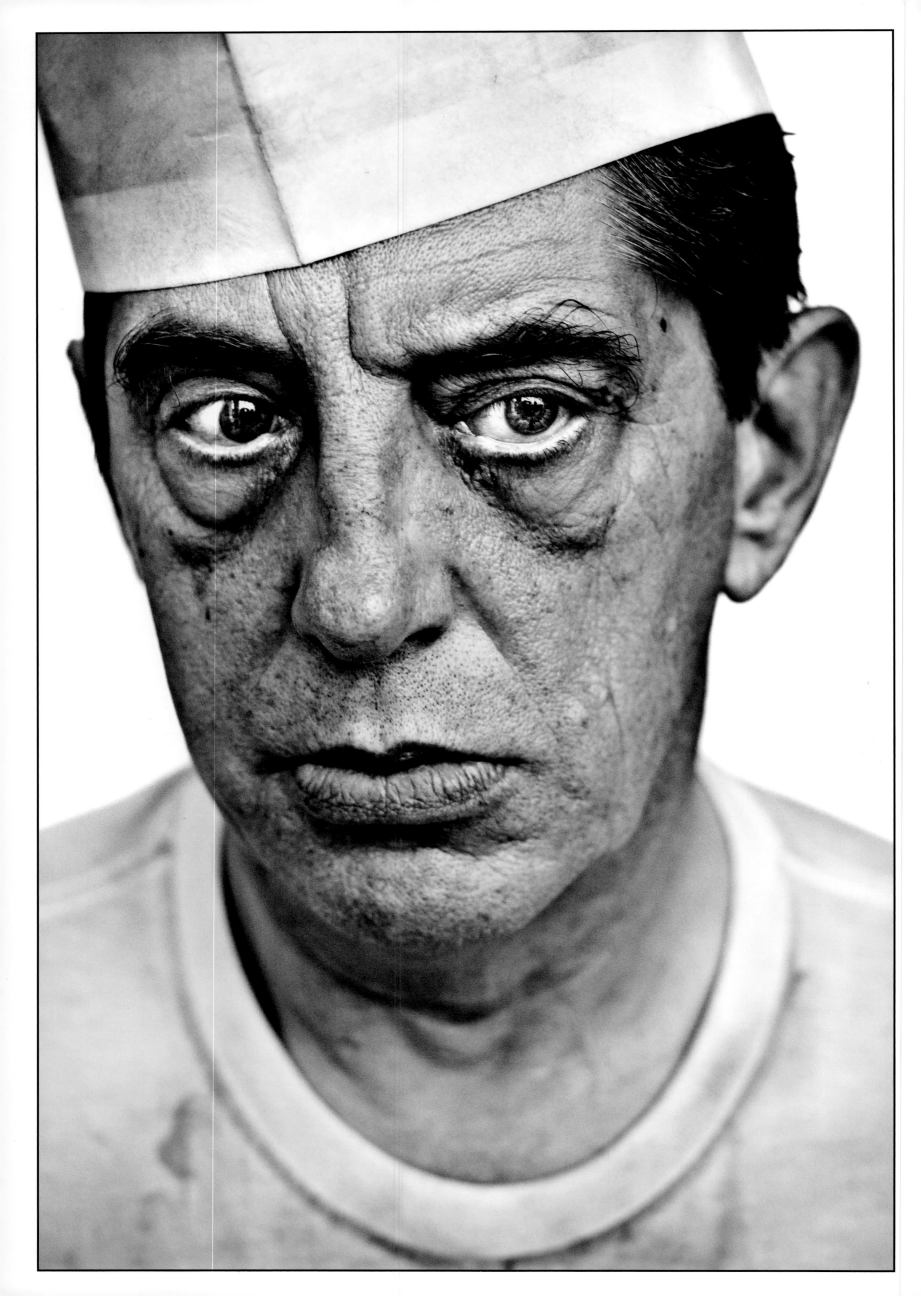

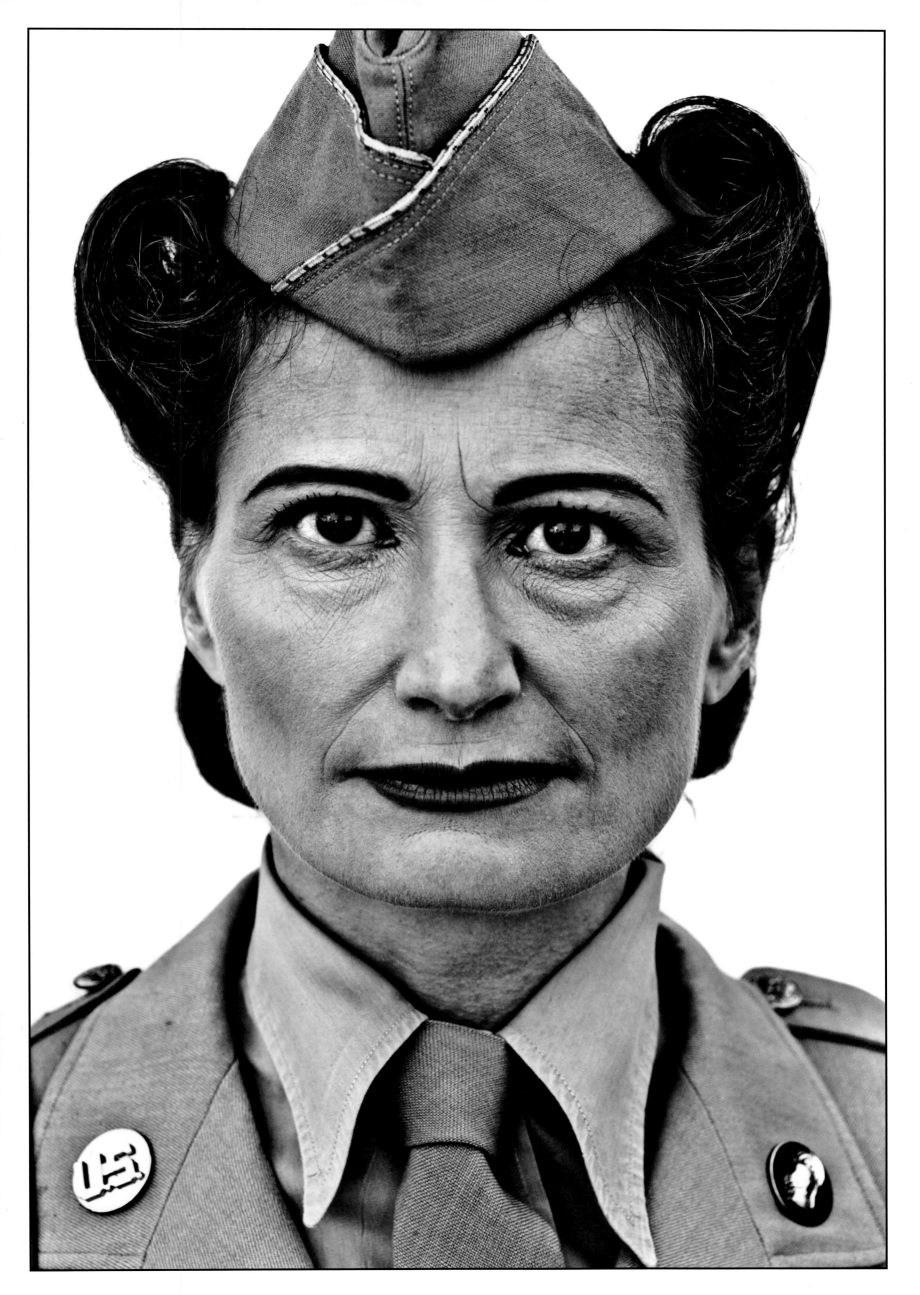

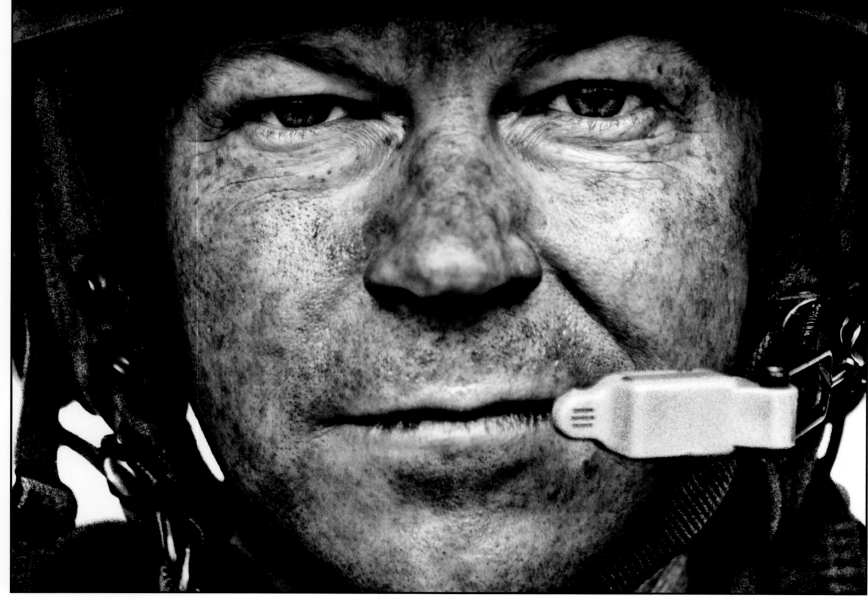

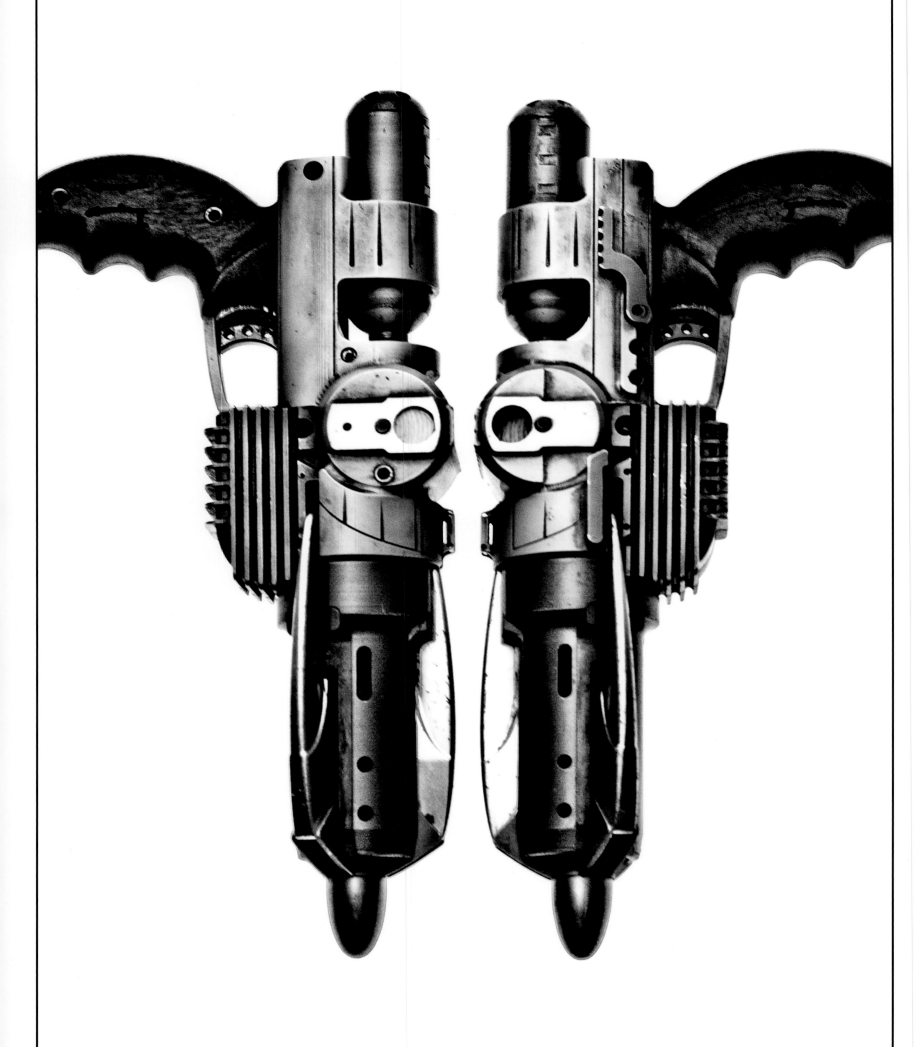

WATCHMENINDEX

Smiley Face Pins

The Comedian

The Comedian's Pistols

1940s Man

Mothman

Disco Woman

Mobster Floosy

Hollis Mason Stunt Double

Hollis Mason

Ad Men

HAZMAT Men

Rioter

New York City Man

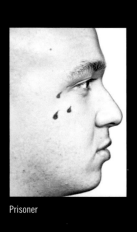

Prisoner

B Dolly Grip

Wally Weaver

Woman at Carnival

Harry's Bar Patron

Rioter

Harry's Bar Patron

New York City Man

Dollar Bill

Prostitute

Executive Producer

Moloch

1940s Woman

Disco Woman

New York City Man

New York City Woman

Bernard the News Vendor

Prop News Clipping

Knot Top

SWAT Cop

Director

Pyramid Delivery Man

Flower Child

Hippie

VJ-Day Soldier

1940s Woman

Young Rorschach

Rorschach Mask

In Gratitude Nite Owl Statue

Young Nite Owl 1

The Comedian

Comedian Stunt Double

Young Bully

Young Bully

1940s Truck Driver

Russian

SPFX Assistant / Rigger

Rioter

Drag Queen

Mothman

Tenement Fire Victim

Tenement Fire Victim

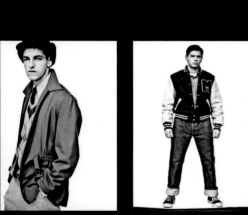

Prop Deep Fryer

Prison Attacker

Prostitute

Rioter

The Comedian

Moloch

Dumb Thug

Fat Thug

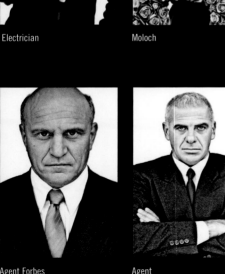

Electrician

Moloch

American Soldiers in Vietnam

American Soldier in Vietnam

Prop Can of Beans

Homeless Man

Agent Forbes

Agent

Seymour

New Frontiersman Editor

Older Sally Jupiter

Inauguration Crowd Member

ison Guard

Prisoner

New York City Man

Times Square Woman

1940s Couple

Young Rorschach
Rorschach's Mother

Gila Flats Cafeteria Woman

Gila Flats Cafeteria Woman

Producer

Prisoner

Walter Kovacs

Big Figure

Dumb Thug
Big Figure
Fat Thug

Soldiers

Wally Weaver

Janey Slater

Aggressive Hooker

Drag Queen

Hooded Justice

Extras Wrangler

Actor portraying Henry Kissinger
Actor portraying Richard Nixon

B Dolly Grip
B Camera Operator

Dr. Manhattan

Visual Effects Supervisor

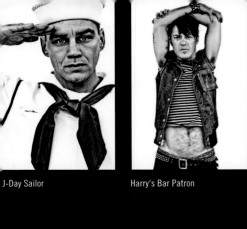

J-Day Sailor

Harry's Bar Patron

Villain

Rioter

Knot Top Costumes

Costume Desginer

Gila Flats Scientist

Man at Carnival

Harry's Bar Patron

Woman at Carnival

Hippie

1950s MP

Rioter

Knot Top Stuntman

Dr. Manhattan

Silk Spectre II

Vietnamese Monk

Vietnamese Girl

Bernie

Veidt Sneakers

New York City Man

1950s Cafeteria Woman

Mobster Floosy

Smiley Face Shirt

not Top Wardrobe

Nixon Inauguration Guest

Rorschach's Costume

Wally Weaver

Captain Metropolis

MP on Campus

Nite Owl

Inauguration Judge

Rioter

Harry's Bar Patron

Actor portraying Annie Leibovitz

Actor portraying Abraham Zaprude

sychiatrist

Walter Kovacs' File

1950s Photographer

1950s Photographer

Talent Driver

Prison Guard Stuntman

Prison Chef

Deli Owner

Actor portraying Fidel Castro

On Set Painter

New York City Woman

Harry's Bar Patron

la Plata Marine

1250s Photographer

Times Square Woman

Unit Production Manager

Production Designer

The Operative

CIA Agent

Actor portraying Dick Cavett

MP on Campus

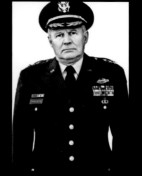
Inauguration Crowd Member

Gila Flats Admiral

Actor portraying Richard Nixon

Rioter

Vietnamese Soldier

Prisoner

VJ-Day Soldier

Disco Woman

Actor portraying David Bowie

Actor portraying Mick Jagger

Moloch

Priest

Adrian Veidt's Assistant

1940s Woman

Rioter

Prisoner

Harry's Bar Patron

Harry's Bar Patron

Psychiatrists

Rioters

Helicopter Pilot in Vietnam

American Soldier in Vietnam

Gunga Diner Hostess

New York City Woman

Rorschach's Grappling Guns

Silhouette

Inauguration Crowd Member

Welder

Stunt Doubles

Sally Jupiter I

Director of Photography

Chief Lighting Technician

Rorschach's Journal

Rorschach